Dad David, Baba Chris and

Written by Ed Merchant

Illustrated by Rachel Fuller

Published by
British Association for Adoption & Fostering
(BAAF)
Saffron House
6-10 Kirby Street
London EC1N 8TS
www.baaf.org.uk

Charity registration 275689 (England and Wales) and SC039337
(Scotland)

Text © Ed Merchant, 2010
Illustrations © Rachel Fuller, 2010

Reprinted 2013, 2014

British Library Cataloguing in Publication Data
A catalogue record for this book is available from the British Library

ISBN 978 1 905664 89 4

Project management by Shaila Shah, Director of Publications, BAAF
Designed and typeset by Helen Joubert Designs
Printed in Great Britain by The Lavenham Press
Trade distribution by Turnaround Publisher Services, Unit 3, Olympia
Trading Estate, Coburg Road, London N22 6TZ

BAAF is the leading UK-wide membership organisation for all those
concerned with adoption, fostering and child care issues.

The author

Ed Merchant began social work in 1967, and has spent several years in child care and child protection, fostering and adoption.

As a gay parent, Ed was aware that there were gay couples who wanted to be parents, and were in a position to offer the emotional and practical care that children need. Some recent research that he did at Anglia Ruskin University convinced Ed that loving parents are what children need, regardless of the parent's gender, and that gay couples needed positive encouragement to put themselves forward.

This book has been written to help and support children who are being parented by gay men, and also as an acknowledgement of the great work that all foster carers and adopters are doing.

The illustrator

Rachel Fuller specialises in children's books and developing and illustrating novelty packages as well as young fiction and educational materials.

Acknowledgements

The author would like to thank Hedi Argent for her invaluable help in the preparation of this little book; Andrew Leary-May, Sarah Borthwick and Chris Christophides for their comments; and Maire Maisch and Patricia Wood, tutors at Anglia Ruskin University, for their support and encouragement to embark on this project.

This book is dedicated to
Lindsay, Leigh, Stefan, Shelly

My Birth

My new family

and to gay dads everywhere

Hi! My name is Ben and I'm nearly eight years old.

I live in an ordinary house, in an ordinary street. I go to an ordinary school and do ordinary things, like playing football and going on the computer.

In fact, I'm just like everybody else.

But I'm not just ordinary, because I have three dads: Dad David and Baba Chris and my birth dad, Alex.

Baba Chris comes from Africa, where fathers are called Baba, so that's what I call him too.

My School

My Computer

My Football Team

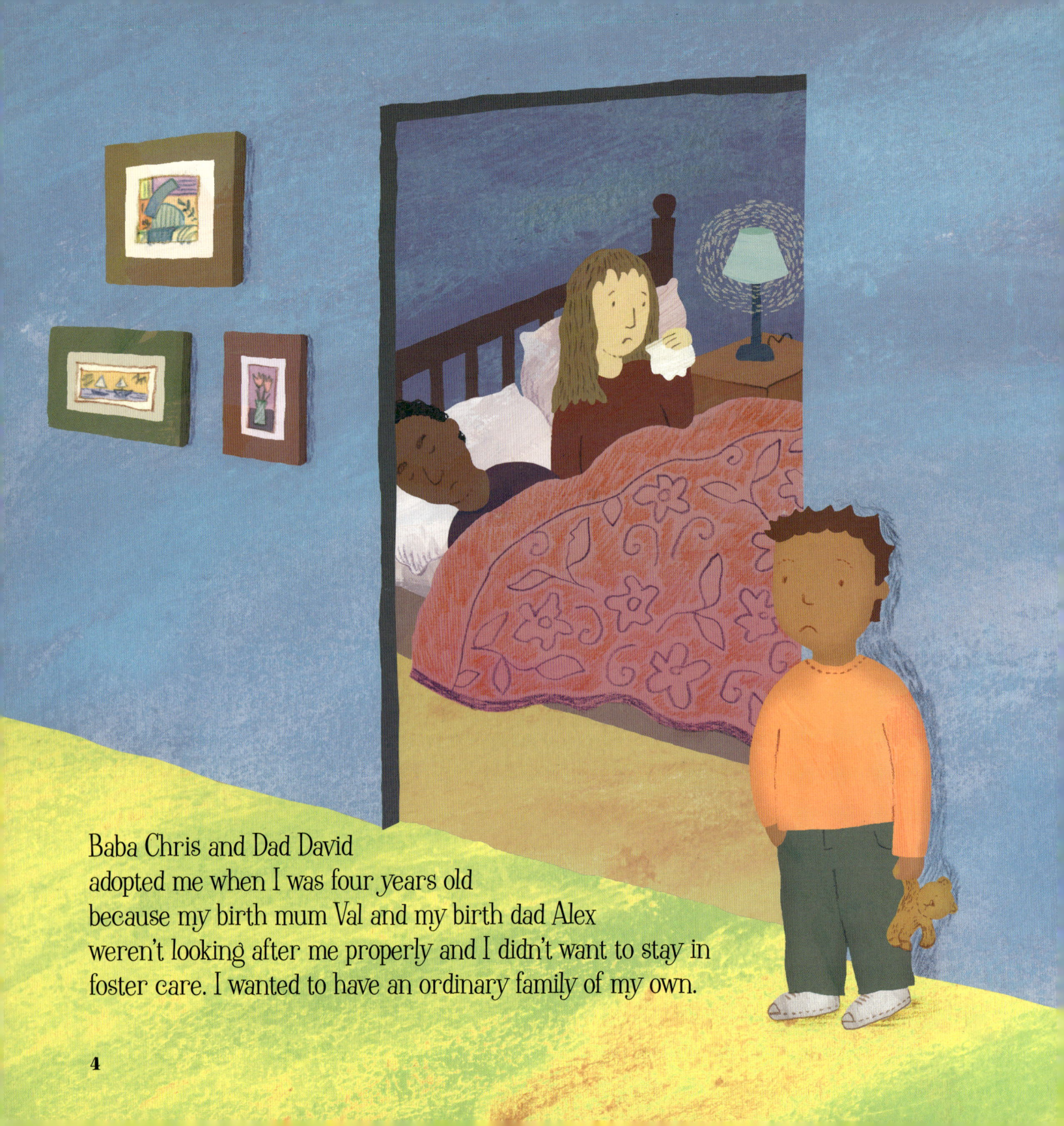

Baba Chris and Dad David
adopted me when I was four years old
because my birth mum Val and my birth dad Alex
weren't looking after me properly and I didn't want to stay in
foster care. I wanted to have an ordinary family of my own.

Dad David

Baba Chris

ME

I was very happy when I went to live with Dad David and Baba Chris. I wanted them to adopt me because they were fun and caring and ordinary.

Dad David is an electrician and Baba Chris works in a hospital. I might be an electrician when I grow up, or I might work in a hospital. Or I might be an artist – I'm good at art.

FURIOUS !

At first I was scared they'd send me away because I used to have temper tantrums, and sometimes, when I got very cross, I'd break things on purpose.

Baba Chris said he understood why I was angry: it was because I'd been moved from one place to another and not had an ordinary family of my own before.

toys

food

Dad David talked to me about my birth mum Val and my birth dad Alex.
I said I often worried about them and wondered how they were.

But Dad David said he knew they were OK or we would have heard and
he promised that when I am older, and if I want, he would help me find
out more about them. I felt much happier again after that.

I stopped getting angry so much and was just ordinary.

My Birth

My new family

When I started junior school, some classmates found out that I lived with two dads. They started teasing me and calling me "gay".

NORMAL ??.

I was very upset when I got home and my dads asked me what was wrong.

I told them what the kids at school were saying because I can tell my two dads everything.

Baba Chris said he would come to school with me the next day.
I started to worry about not being ordinary any more.
I didn't want to be different from everybody else.

Next day Baba Chris took me to
school, and we had a chat with my
teacher.

Miss Patel was very kind and told
me that children live in all kinds of
families.

Some live with a mum and dad, but
some only have a mum or a dad.
Some have two mums or two dads.

Khaled's
Mum & Dad

Leyla's Mum

Some children live with their grandparents or their aunts and uncles, and some children live with foster carers or in a children's home.

Rosa's Grandparents

She said everyone is different and no one is just ordinary because every child and every family are also special.

Miss Patel said that if children are loved and cared for, it doesn't matter who they live with.

Miss Patel made me feel special and I didn't mind not just being ordinary any more.

Miss Patel said it was very wrong of my classmates to tease me about my dads being gay. She said they hadn't learnt that being gay meant that two dads could love each other just like their mums and dads did.

That all seems a long time ago now, but the name-calling hasn't really stopped.

It used to make me feel hurt and lonely, but now I just feel sorry for the children who don't understand that being different is special.

I do have some good friends at school who are very kind, and they are the ones I invite to my birthday parties.

I think it's great to live with two dads. I know Baba Chris and Dad David love each other and they love me and I love them.

It all feels quite ordinary, but I'm glad it also feels special. Me and my dads make a great family.

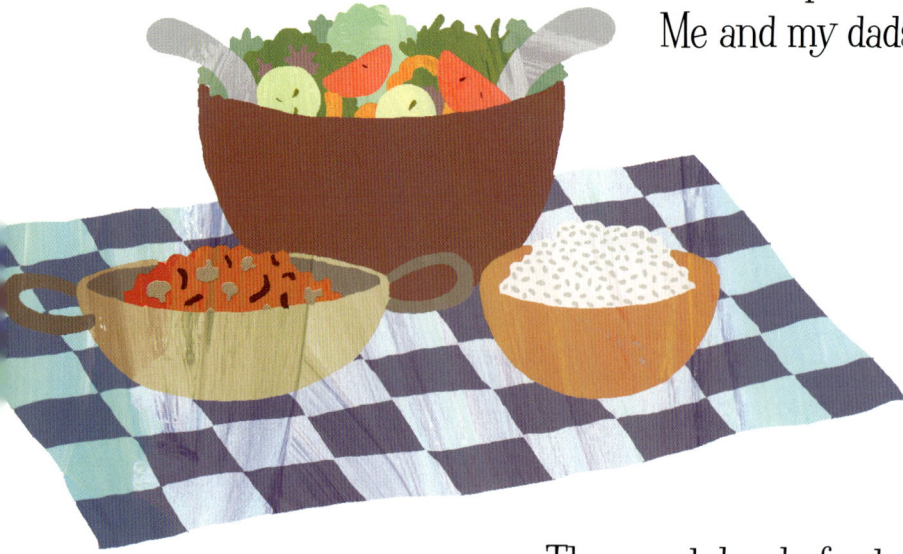

They cook lovely food and we all go shopping together. I never miss school and they help me with my homework whenever I'm stuck.

When I play football for the school, they come and cheer me on.

If I'm not well, they always take me to the doctor.

Auntie Laura & cousins Finn & Ella

Sometimes we have trips to the beach with my grandma and grandpa and my aunties and uncles and cousins.

ME and my Dads

Grandpa Joe

Last year we went on holiday to Spain, and we're saving up to go to Disneyworld next year.

And I haven't had a temper tantrum for ages.

15

One day I asked my dads if they thought I would grow up gay like them.

Baba Chris said that when I was older, I would know just how I felt, and I could always talk to them about it.

Dad David said I would most likely find a girlfriend. They both said it would be quite alright and quite ordinary whatever I did.

But it would be special for me.

I sometimes think about what I will be when I grow up.

My dads say I can be and do anything as long as I'm kind and caring.

The other day I asked my dads if I could have a brother or sister. I wonder what having a brother or sister will be like?

They said they would ask the adoption people about that; the same people who found my special family for me.

I would love to have a brother or sister or both. I hope they'll be ordinary just like me, and then I'll be able to tell them they're also special!